Deserts
INSIDE OUT

Marina Cohen

CRABTREE
Publishing Company
www.crabtreebooks.com

Author: Marina Cohen
**Publishing plan research
    and series development:** Reagan Miller
Editorial director: Kathy Middleton
Editors: Sarah Eason, Jennifer Sanderson,
    Nancy Dickmann, and Shirley Duke
Proofreader: Wendy Scavuzzo
Project coordinator: Sarah Eason
Design: Paul Myerscough
Photo research: Rachel Blount
**Production coordinator and
    Prepress technician:** Tammy McGarr
Print coordinator: Katherine Berti

Written, developed, and produced by Calcium

Library and Archives Canada Cataloguing in Publication

Cohen, Marina, author
    Deserts inside out / Marina Cohen.

(Ecosystems inside out)
Includes index.
Issued in print and electronic formats.
ISBN 978-0-7787-0627-4 (bound).--
ISBN 978-0-7787-0673-1 (pbk.).--
ISBN 978-1-4271-7646-2 (pdf).--
ISBN 978-1-4271-7640-0 (html)

    1. Desert ecology--Juvenile literature. 2. Desert animals--
Juvenile literature. I. Title.

QH541.5.D4C64 2014   j577.54   C2014-903623-X
                                          C2014-903624-8

Library of Congress Cataloging-in-Publication Data

Cohen, Marina, 1967-
 Deserts inside out / Marina Cohen.
    pages cm. -- (Ecosystems inside out)
 Includes index.
 ISBN 978-0-7787-0627-4 (reinforced library binding) -- ISBN 978-0-7787-0673-1 (pbk.) --
 ISBN 978-1-4271-7646-2 (electronic pdf) --
 ISBN 978-1-4271-7640-0 (electronic html)
 1. Desert ecology--Juvenile literature 2. Deserts--Juvenile literature. I. Title.

 QH541.5.D4C64 2015
 577.54--dc23
                                          2014020252

Crabtree Publishing Company

www.crabtreebooks.com   1-800-387-7650

Printed in Hong Kong/082014/BK20140613

**Published in Canada
Crabtree Publishing**
616 Welland Ave.
St. Catharines, Ontario
L2M 5V6

**Published in the United States
Crabtree Publishing**
PMB 59051
350 Fifth Avenue, 59th Floor
New York, New York 10118

**Published in the United Kingdom
Crabtree Publishing**
Maritime House
Basin Road North, Hove
BN41 1WR

**Published in Australia
Crabtree Publishing**
3 Charles Street
Coburg North
VIC, 3058

Contents

What Is an Ecosystem?

Our planet, Earth, is home to many living things. All plants and animals depend on other living things, as well as nonliving things, to survive. Living things are called **biotic factors**. Nonliving things are called **abiotic factors**. They include sunshine, water, air, temperature, and soil. An **ecosystem** is made up of **organisms**, the environment in which they live, and their **interrelationships**.

Sizes of Ecosystems

Ecosystems can be large or small. For example, a puddle can be an ecosystem. A **biome** is a large geographical area that contains similar plants, animals, and environments. Rain forests, grasslands, tundras, oceans, and deserts are biomes.

What Is a Desert?

The word "desert" means "an abandoned place." Yet deserts are home to many plants and animals that are able to survive the harsh desert **climate**. Deserts get very little rain, so the climate is dry. There are hot deserts, such as the Sahara, and cold deserts, such as Antarctica. Hot deserts are very hot during the day, but temperatures are much cooler at night.

Let's explore some desert ecosystems around the world, then zoom in on one specific part of them.

What Is a System?

A **system** is a group of separate parts that work together for a purpose. An ecosystem helps ensure the survival of its living parts. Sunshine, water, soil, plants, insects, and animals are some of the parts of an ecosystem. Each abiotic and biotic part has a specific and important role to play that helps the ecosystem function.

Healthy ecosystems have many different types of plants and animals that live together, all having their specific needs met. Ecosystems work in a delicate balance—even a small change in an ecosystem can affect all the parts within it.

Key

- Deserts
- Grasslands
- Oceans
- Rain forests
- Tundras
- Wetlands

This map shows where deserts and other biomes are found around the world.

One fifth of Earth's land surface is covered in desert.

Energy in Ecosystems

sun

Every living thing in an ecosystem needs **energy** to survive. Energy comes from food. A **food chain** shows how an organism gets food, and how this energy is then passed from one organism to another. Many different organisms rely on just one food chain.

Jobs in a Food Chain

Living things in an ecosystem can be producers, consumers, or decomposers. The sun gives energy to plants so they can grow. Plants are called producers because they make their own food through a process called **photosynthesis**.

Animals are consumers. They need to eat other living things to get energy to survive. Herbivores eat plants. Carnivores are meat-eaters. Some carnivores eat herbivores, while others eat carnivores. Omnivores eat plants and animals.

Decomposers, such as **fungi** and **bacteria**, live off dead plants and animals. They are nature's recyclers—they break down dead organisms and put **nutrients** back into the soil or water so the food chain can begin again.

Food Webs

Every living thing is connected in many ways to other living things, so a better term for the flow of energy between organisms is a **food web**. A healthy food web meets the needs of many different **species**. It contains several overlapping food chains. A healthy food web makes use of **native** species. Healthy food webs begin with plenty of sunshine, good quality soil, and a lot of water.

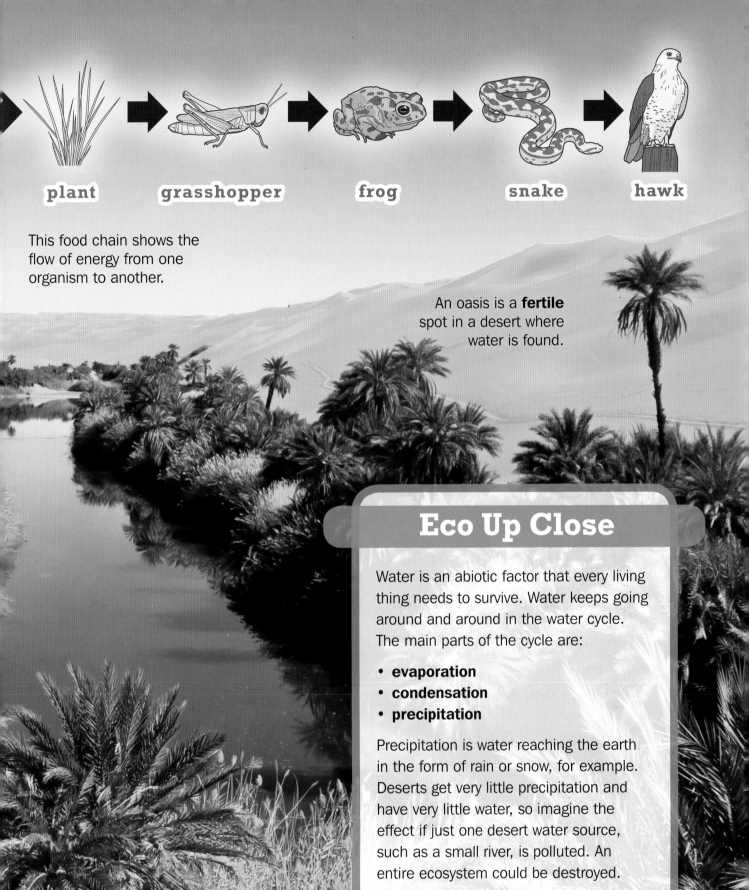

plant → **grasshopper** → **frog** → **snake** → **hawk**

This food chain shows the flow of energy from one organism to another.

An oasis is a **fertile** spot in a desert where water is found.

Eco Up Close

Water is an abiotic factor that every living thing needs to survive. Water keeps going around and around in the water cycle. The main parts of the cycle are:

- **evaporation**
- **condensation**
- **precipitation**

Precipitation is water reaching the earth in the form of rain or snow, for example. Deserts get very little precipitation and have very little water, so imagine the effect if just one desert water source, such as a small river, is polluted. An entire ecosystem could be destroyed.

The Sahara Desert

Africa's largest desert, the Sahara, is one of the hottest deserts in the world! It is also very dry and extremely windy. Organisms that live in the Sahara can survive on very little water, which they mostly get from the food they eat. Plants such as fig trees, olive trees, date palms, grasses, cacti, and shrubs grow in the Sahara. They provide food for herbivores, such as Cape hares, dama gazelles, antelopes, and jerboas.

Symbiotic Relationships

Symbiosis is a special relationship between different species, which provides at least one of them with nutrition. There are different types of symbiotic relationships.

Parasitism

Leeches are **parasites**. They attach themselves to animals such as crocodiles and feed on their blood. The leech benefits by getting food, but it can harm the crocodile by infecting it with diseases.

Mutualism

The Egyptian plover and the Nile crocodile have a **mutualistic** relationship. The crocodile opens its mouth and the bird enters it to feed on leeches. Both bird and crocodile benefit from this relationship. The bird finds food, and the teeth and mouth of the crocodile are cleaned.

Commensalism

By eating the waste of other animals, the dung beetle gets nutrition. That relationship is known as commensalism. The dung beetle benefits from other animals, while they are neither helped nor harmed by it.

Predation

Predators hunt and kill other organisms for food. Sand vipers, scorpions, and monitor lizards are some of the predators in the Sahara. Spotted hyenas, Saharan cheetahs, and desert eagle owls are apex predators. Apex predators have few, or no predators, other than humans.

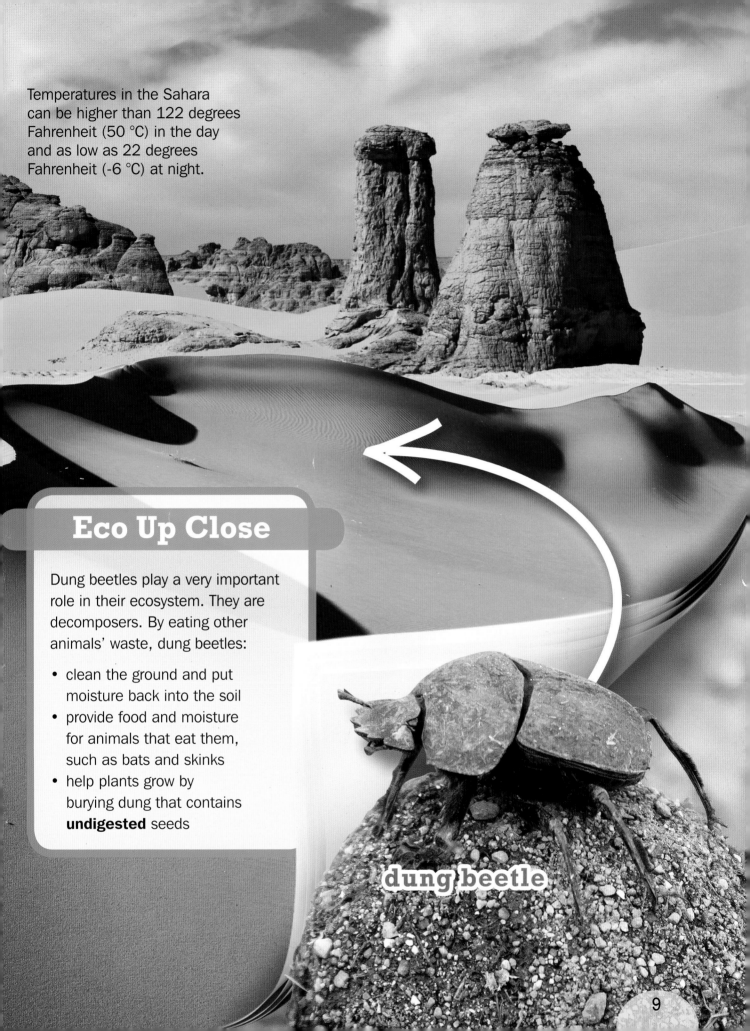

Temperatures in the Sahara can be higher than 122 degrees Fahrenheit (50 °C) in the day and as low as 22 degrees Fahrenheit (-6 °C) at night.

Eco Up Close

Dung beetles play a very important role in their ecosystem. They are decomposers. By eating other animals' waste, dung beetles:

- clean the ground and put moisture back into the soil
- provide food and moisture for animals that eat them, such as bats and skinks
- help plants grow by burying dung that contains **undigested** seeds

dung beetle

The Mojave Desert

The dry, windy Mojave Desert is found in the southwestern United States. Joshua trees, Mojave sage, and mesquite trees are some of the plant life found in this desert, but the main plant is creosote.

Creosote

With special leaves that keep in moisture, a creosote bush has one long root that reaches water deep under the ground. It also has shallow roots that can suck up any rain that falls on the surface. A creosote bush provides food and shelter for many organisms. One example is the walking stick insect. **Adaptations** have helped this insect blend right in to its home. Adapting means changing, over generations, to better suit the environment. The walking stick looks exactly like a creosote leaf when it first hatches and a creosote twig when it is an adult. This adaptation helps the insect hide from predators. Jackrabbits and desert iguanas eat creosote leaves, while desert woodrats and kangaroo rats depend on creosote seeds for food. These rats also shelter in the bush's roots.

Best Friends Forever!

The yucca plant has a mutualistic relationship with the yucca moth. The moth's **larvae** depend on the seeds of the yucca plant for food, and only the moth can **pollinate** the yucca plant.

Joshua trees grow only in the Mojave Desert. They can live for more than 150 years!

Eco Up Close

The desert tortoise is a keystone species in the Mojave Desert. A keystone species is one that plays such an important role in its environment that it affects other organisms. Other animals hide from predators and harsh weather inside tortoise **burrows**. When tortoises excrete their wastes, they spread seeds from the plants they eat. New plants grow from the seeds, which **repopulate** the ecosystem.

desert tortoise

Eco Focus

Solar farms and wind farms use renewable sources of energy to make power. There are several of these farms in the Mojave Desert. Although they provide "clean" energy, they also destroy the **habitat** of organisms such as the desert tortoise. Are the benefits to Earth's environment from green energy more important than the loss of animal homes? Explain your thinking and support your answer using evidence from the book.

The Gobi Desert

The Gobi is Asia's largest desert. It covers parts of China and Mongolia. Temperatures can drop to -40 degrees Fahrenheit (-40 °C) in the winter and rise to 113 degrees Fahrenheit (45 °C) in the summer. Sometimes the temperature shifts from really hot to really cold in just one day! The landscape is mostly rock, with some grasslands, sandy areas, mountains, and **salt ponds**.

The Gobi Food Web

Hardy plants are found at the bottom of many food webs. In the Gobi, saxaul trees, wild onions, and ephedra provide food for gazelles, geckos, and jerboas. Golden eagles **prey on** the jerboas and the geckos, while snow leopards hunt gazelles.

Sucking Up Water

Mining can destroy ecosystems by polluting animal homes and draining precious resources such as water. The Gobi was one of Earth's great **wilderness** areas until mining companies opened pits and dug up huge amounts of coal. In an already dry climate, mining uses up precious water needed by organisms that live in the desert. Roads to mines have damaged grasslands. Mining vehicles churn up dust, harming plants and animals. Plants coated with dust cannot carry out photosynthesis and dust interferes with animals' vision, breathing and food sources for herbivores, too. If mining is not controlled, the Gobi ecosystem could be destroyed.

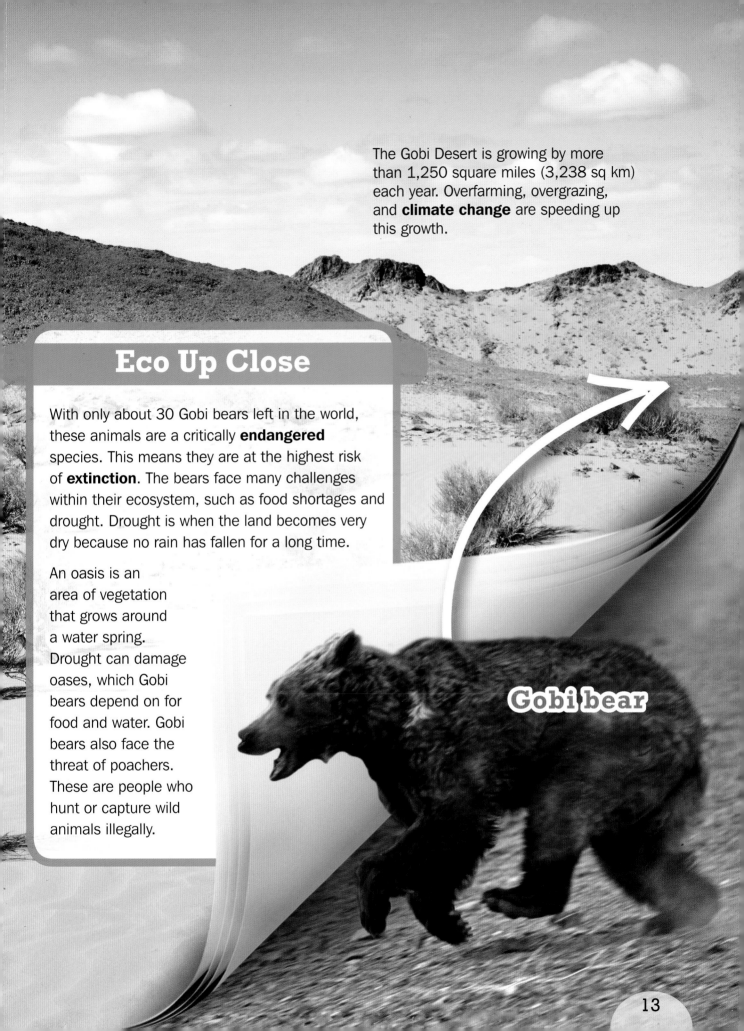

The Gobi Desert is growing by more than 1,250 square miles (3,238 sq km) each year. Overfarming, overgrazing, and **climate change** are speeding up this growth.

Eco Up Close

With only about 30 Gobi bears left in the world, these animals are a critically **endangered** species. This means they are at the highest risk of **extinction**. The bears face many challenges within their ecosystem, such as food shortages and drought. Drought is when the land becomes very dry because no rain has fallen for a long time.

An oasis is an area of vegetation that grows around a water spring. Drought can damage oases, which Gobi bears depend on for food and water. Gobi bears also face the threat of poachers. These are people who hunt or capture wild animals illegally.

Gobi bear

The Chihuahuan Desert

Located mainly in Mexico, the Chihuahuan Desert is the largest desert in North America. Small mountains run through it, with valleys and rivers between them. There are many streams, lakes, and **arroyos** that form during the rainy summers. After the rainy season, the Chihuahuan Desert has more water than most deserts, so it is home to many animals, such as fish and turtles, and many plants, such as cacti.

Taking Too Much

Some people collect rare and even threatened species of cacti. They use them as garden plants, for food, or for medicine. This action contributes to the overharvesting of some cacti that grow wild in the Chihuahuan Desert. Overharvesting means using up a natural resource faster than it can be replaced.

Needing One Another

All organisms rely on other organisms, as well as on abiotic factors. For example, in the Chihuahuan Desert, milkweed depends on soil, sunshine, rain, and air to make its own food and to grow. It also depends on insects, such as butterflies, moths, and bees, to pollinate it. Monarch caterpillars depend on milkweed leaves for food and shelter. Monarch butterflies depend on the plant's nectar for food. The way in which organisms rely on each other is called **interdependence**.

The beautiful landscape of the Chihuahuan Desert is threatened by increasing human settlements, and their poor use of water and bad cattle management.

Eco Focus

Desert plants can survive with very little water. To save water, some cities, such as Phoenix and Tucson, are using desert plants in their **landscaping**. Many of these plants are taken directly from the desert. Do you think it is okay to solve a problem in our cities if it creates a problem in other ecosystems? Explain your thinking.

Eco Up Close

The soapberry hairstreak is a butterfly that lives around the soapberry tree. Soapberry hairstreak caterpillars eat only soapberry tree leaves. The caterpillars change into butterflies at the exact same time that the soapberry tree grows flowers. This allows the butterflies to feed on nectar from the flowers. Birds, snakes, toads, lizards, and ants eat the caterpillars and butterflies. All these organisms are interdependent.

soapberry hairstreak

The Atacama Desert

The Atacama Desert in northern Chile is one of the driest places on Earth. Only Antarctica is drier. Although some areas of the desert get moisture from fog, many have never seen a drop of rain! Very few plants and animals have adapted to this extreme environment. Parts of the desert are almost lifeless. With no decomposers, such as fungi and bacteria, some dead plants have not decomposed for thousands of years!

Depending on Each Other

The plants and animals that survive in the Atacama depend greatly on each other. For example, algae and fungi are two interdependent organisms that join together to form **lichens**. This is another example of mutualism. Shrubs and lichens provide food and shelter for a few insects and small **mammals**, such as myotis bats and manso grass mice. Several types of birds visit the fog areas of the desert to feed on insects.

Slowly Becoming Deserts

Desertification is the changing of land into a desert. Some areas in the world are slowly becoming deserts, but deserts themselves are also growing. There are many causes of desertification. One cause is a shift in climate. If the climate becomes hotter and drier, the land becomes less fertile, and plants can no longer grow in it. Due to desertification, the Atacama is one of the five most endangered regions in the world. This means the few living things that exist there will die out.

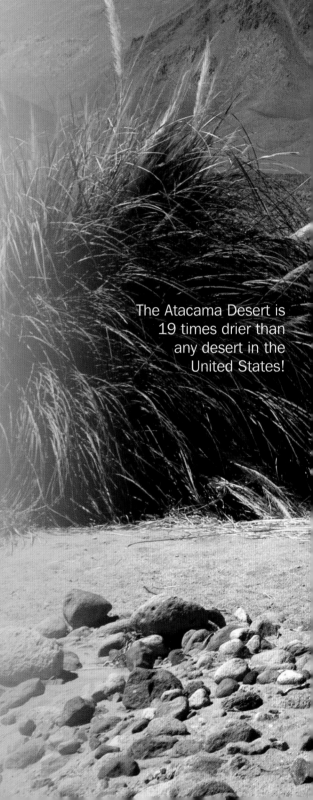

The Atacama Desert is 19 times drier than any desert in the United States!

16

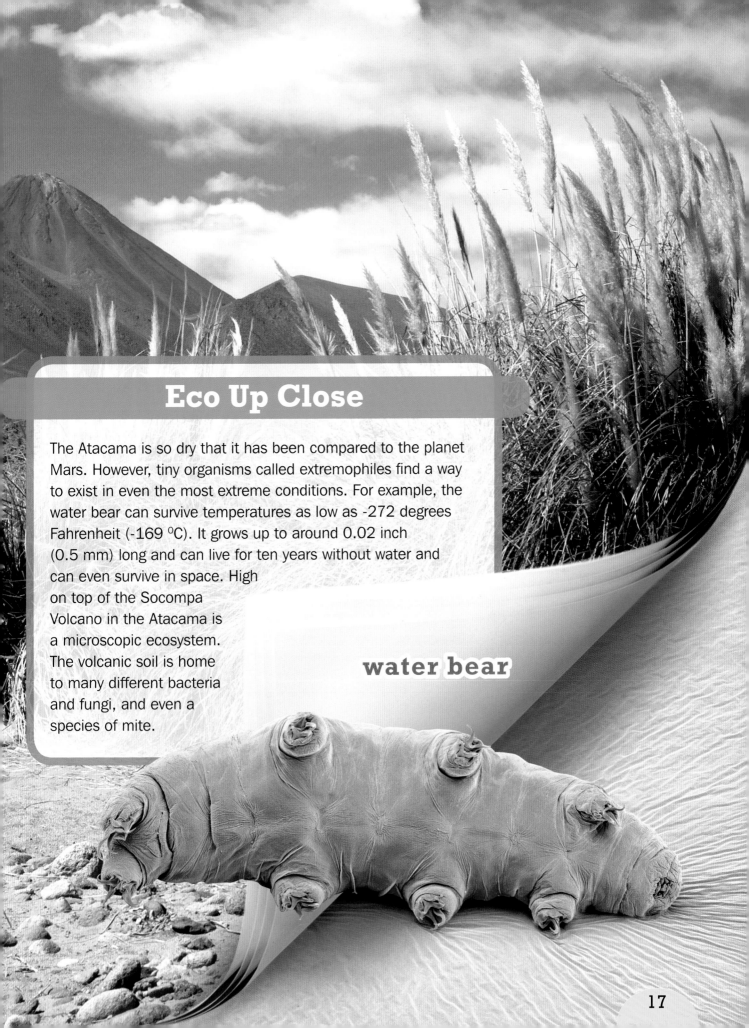

Eco Up Close

The Atacama is so dry that it has been compared to the planet Mars. However, tiny organisms called extremophiles find a way to exist in even the most extreme conditions. For example, the water bear can survive temperatures as low as -272 degrees Fahrenheit (-169 $^\circ$C). It grows up to around 0.02 inch (0.5 mm) long and can live for ten years without water and can even survive in space. High on top of the Socompa Volcano in the Atacama is a microscopic ecosystem. The volcanic soil is home to many different bacteria and fungi, and even a species of mite.

water bear

The Sonoran Desert

The Sonoran Desert is located in parts of Mexico, Arizona, and California. It gets more rain than any other desert. When it rains, the Sonoran is damp and cool. Other times, it is hot and dry.

Survival Tactics

Like all desert plants, those in the Sonoran Desert have different ways to survive, or adaptations. Some plants, such as owl's clover, change their **life cycles** so that they live only when the environment is healthy. If the environment becomes unhealthy, the plant disappears. The roots and seeds are dormant. When conditions are healthy again, the roots and seeds become active and the plant reappears. Other plants, such as the saguaro cactus and hedgehog cactus, store water so they are able to live all year.

Eating Too Much

When animals, such as cows or sheep, are allowed to eat plants right down to their roots, the plants die. This is called overgrazing. This is one of the main causes of desertification in the Sonoran Desert. Grasses and other plant roots hold soil together. Without them, the soil loosens and is blown away. This causes the **erosion** of topsoil that new plants need to grow.

Off-Roading

Small actions can disturb the balance in an ecosystem. Riding through the desert in a jeep, on a motorcycle, or on another all-terrain vehicle may seem to be fun, but it can damage ecosystems because it crushes or kills fragile plant life. This is why off-roading has been outlawed in the Sonoran Desert.

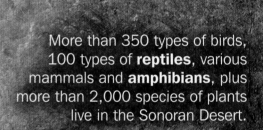

More than 350 types of birds, 100 types of **reptiles**, various mammals and **amphibians**, plus more than 2,000 species of plants live in the Sonoran Desert.

Eco Up Close

The saguaro cactus has several symbiotic relationships. It provides food and shelter for many living things. It can store more than 40 gallons (151 liters) of rain, so many insects and animals depend on the saguaro cactus for food and water. The long-nosed bat, bees, wasps, ants, and butterflies drink the nectar of its flowers. Pack rats and pocket mice eat its flesh. Gila woodpeckers hollow out the inside of the cactus and make their nest there. The woodpecker eats insects that could harm the cactus.

gila woodpecker

saguaro cactus

The Great Sandy Desert

Of the ten deserts in Australia, the Great Sandy Desert is the second largest. For a desert, it gets a surprising amount of rain. However, the rainwater evaporates very quickly in the desert heat, leaving the land extremely dry.

Tough and Spiky

The main plant in the Great Sandy Desert is spinifex. It is a tough, spiky-leaved grass that provides shelter for princess parrots, Mulga parrots, and scarlet-chested parrots, as well as various lizards and snakes. Its seeds provide food for birds and other organisms.

Not-So-Pleased to Meet You!

Invasive species are animals or plants that are not native to a particular area. This means that they are not usually found there. Humans or other forces may have introduced invasive organisms to the ecosystem. Invasive species often compete for food and shelter with native species. They can harm ecosystems and cause the extinction of native organisms by taking away their food, water, or nesting sites as they out-compete native life.

The introduction of cats and foxes to the Great Sandy Desert has harmed native species. Cats and foxes feed on native animals, such as bilbies. They also threaten lizards by out-competing them for food. Red foxes can have **mange**. Mange is a skin disease caused by parasitic mites. This disease has threatened native wombats and dingoes.

The Great Sandy Desert is part of a larger desert area known as the Western Desert. The sand in the desert is red in color.

Eco Up Close

Termites are decomposers. They play an important role in the recycling of dead plants. Though most organisms cannot digest spinifex, termites thrive on it. Although termites cannot digest the plant themselves, the **microorganisms** that live inside a termites' stomach can. Termites have a mutualistic relationship with microorganisms. The termite eats the plant. The microorganisms help break it down. In this way, both organisms get food.

termite

The Kalahari Desert

The Kalahari is located in southern Africa. Certain areas of the desert get too much rain for it to be called a true desert, but rain in the area is very unpredictable. Part of the Kalahari is covered in grassland.

Small Is Beautiful

Although some trees, such as camel thorn and black thorn, have adapted to the climate, small plants, such as devil's claw, grow best in the Kalahari. The hoodia cactus loves the dry climate. Its flowers smell like rotten meat. This protects the cactus by keeping hungry animals away. The smell attracts flies that lay eggs in rotting meat. The flies help the hoodia cactus by pollinating it so that it can make seeds and **reproduce**.

Just Hanging Out

The red-billed oxpecker and the giraffe have a mutualistic relationship. Ticks, horseflies, and other parasites live on the giraffe. Their constant bites can be annoying but, worse still, they can infect the giraffe with disease. The oxpecker sits on the giraffe and feeds on the parasites. This relationship benefits both animals—the bird finds food and the giraffe gets rid of pests.

Dangers of Overhunting

Many animals in the Kalahari, such as lions, cheetahs, and hyenas, are endangered species. One of the reasons for this is overhunting. In exchange for small amounts of money, poachers hunt and kill these animals illegally to sell their skins or their body parts for traditional medicine.

Some people believe the Kalahari Desert gets its name from the Tswana word *Kgala* which means "great thirst."

Eco Up Close

Meerkats live in groups called "mobs" or "gangs." They are omnivores. Though they mainly eat insects, spiders, and millipedes, they also eat fungi, such as the kalaharituber, small mammals, and eggs. Meerkats are **immune** to some types of **venom**, so they can eat scorpions and snakes without being harmed. This helps keep the desert snake **population** under control. Meerkats share their burrow with yellow mongooses and ground squirrels because they do not compete with these animals for food.

meerkat

The Arabian Desert

The Arabian Desert covers most of Saudi Arabia and stretches into Jordan, Iraq, Kuwait, Qatar, the United Arab Emirates, Oman, and Yemen. Oil and gas are found beneath the desert's surface. It is extremely dry and is home to the largest area of sand in the world. Although only a few plants are able to survive in the desert's harsh climate, those that do have adapted quite well.

The Arabian Desert is the second largest hot desert in the world.

Life-Saving Trees

Plants in the Arabian Desert include caper, ghaf, juniper, and date palms. Sedge, a grasslike plant with deep roots, also grows well in the sandy soil. Tamarisk trees are found near the borders of natural springs that form oases. These trees help protect the water by forming a natural barrier that keeps the desert sand from the water. Without the trees, sand would fill the spring, and it would dry up. Without the spring's water, the plants, insects, and animals that depend on it would not be able to survive.

Eco Focus

Ecosystems in the Arabian and Syrian deserts have been threatened by the construction of oil and gas pipelines. What do people use gas and oil for? Research alternative energy sources. Which would you recommend people use to reduce the destruction of desert ecosystems?

Eco Up Close

When certain organisms such as beetles and rodents get out of control, the balance of an ecosystem is threatened. These pests can eat too many plants or may carry diseases. Luckily, nature has its own pest controllers, such as the camel spider. Camel spiders are **nocturnal** and hide in burrows or beneath rocks during the day. At night, they hunt darkling beetles, termites, centipedes, spiders, and scorpions. They can also feed on rodents, snakes, and small lizards. Camel spiders are an important part of their ecosystem because they keep pest populations under control. Vultures, eagles, and other large birds eat camel spiders, keeping their numbers in check.

camel spider

25

Antarctica

Antarctica is the coldest and the windiest **continent** on Earth. Antarctica's water is frozen, which makes it the driest place in the world and a polar desert. Mosses, fungi, and algae live in Antarctica. Even ancient bacteria ecosystems exist deep beneath its **glaciers**!

Alive Again!

Microscopic mites, nematodes, and springtails are able to survive the harsh conditions by miraculously "dying" then coming back to life! When conditions get too dry, nematodes go into a death-like state. Months—or even decades—later, when conditions improve, they spring back to life. These organisms feed on fungi and bacteria.

Perfect for Penguins

Some types of penguins breed in Antarctica. They play an important role in the ecosystem because their eggs and chicks provide food for birds called South Polar skuas. By eating the eggs and some chicks, Skuas help keep the penguin populations under control. Skuas also prey on snow petrels. Snow petrels are birds that feed mainly on fish and krill, but they also help the ecosystem by eating dead animals.

Climate Change

The increase in the average temperature on Earth is called climate change and it is causing sea ice in Antarctica to melt. **Phytoplankton** lives on the bottom of sea ice. It makes its food in a similar way to plants, so it is a producer. If it disappears, so does food for organisms such as krill.

Penguins have adaptations that protect them from the cold. They have thick skin and lots of fat that help them stay warm. When it is really cold, they huddle in large groups.

Eco Focus

Certain areas of the ocean lack phytoplankton. Without phytoplankton, the whole food web suffers. One of the causes of the decrease in phytoplankton is climate change. Research the causes of climate change. What could you do to help stop climate change? Explain your thinking.

Eco Up Close

Krill are small sea creatures that are around just 2.4 inches (6 cm) long. They are the keystone species of Antarctica because so many other organisms depend on them for food. Antarctic krill eat phytoplankton and ice algae. These organisms are then eaten by whales, seals, squid, penguins, fish, albatrosses, and many types of birds.

krill

Don't Desert Our Deserts!

Deserts cover about one fifth of the land on our planet. Despite their reputations of being dry wastelands, they are home to many unique organisms that can only survive within them. If even one species of plant or animal becomes extinct, it will affect many others. The survival and well-being of ecosystems depends on everyone—and that includes you!

What Can You Do?

Do not dump oil, pesticides, detergents, or paint into storm drains, from which these pollutants can travel to ecosystems.

Reduce waste by asking yourself questions about what you or your family buy. Is the product made with environmentally friendly materials? Does the company use too much packaging? Can you dispose of the product in a way that will not harm the environment?

Protect the environment and wildlife. Do not use pesticides or chemicals on your lawns. Plant only native species in your backyard. Never release a plant or animal species into an area where it does not naturally exist. Do not buy souvenirs made from wildlife.

Educate others by starting or joining an Eco-Club in your school. Write an Eco-Blog.

Activity:

Create an Energy Pyramid!

Each organism plays an important role in its ecosystem. One aspect of this is an organism's place in the food web. Create your own desert energy pyramid to discover what eats what!

You Will Need:

- Construction paper
- Pictures of specific plants and animals— look for these on the Internet and print them out to make your model
- Glue
- Markers

Instructions

The sample chart below shows one organism from each level of a desert energy pyramid. Using the chart and researching a particular desert, create a pyramid demonstrating the feeding relationship of some of the organisms in it. Label the desert being represented, as well as all the animals and plants. Include more than one organism on each level below the top.

	apex predator (predator with few or no predators)
	**tertiary consumer** (carnivore that eats other carnivores)
	**secondary consumer** (carnivore that eats herbivores)
	primary consumer (herbivore)
	**primary producer** (plant)
	**decomposer** (breaks down dead plants and animals)

The Challenge

Once your pyramid is complete, present it to others and discuss the following questions:

- How might a change on one level affect all other levels?
- Why are there more organisms on the bottom level than on the top?
- Think about how with each level you go up, you lose more of the original energy from the sun.

Glossary

Please note: Some bold-faced words are defined in the text

abiotic factors Nonliving parts of an ecosystem, such as water and soil

amphibians Animals, such as frogs, that begin life in water then live on land as adults

arroyos Streams that are usually dry except after heavy rain

bacteria Living organisms made up of one cell

biotic factors Living parts of an ecosystem, such as plants and animals

burrows Holes or tunnels in the ground made by animals for shelter

climate The usual weather in a specific area

climate change A process in which the environment changes to become warmer, colder, drier, or wetter than normal. This can occur naturally, or it can be caused by human activity

condensation The process in which water vapor cools and changes to liquid form

continent A landmass, or large area of land, such as North America, Asia, or Australia

desertification The loss of plant life and soil at the boundaries of a desert caused by drought and overgrazing

ecosystem A group of living and nonliving things that live and interact in an area

endangered At risk of dying out

energy The ability to do work

erosion The process in which soil and rocks are worn away by wind and water over time

evaporation The process in which water is heated by the sun and changed from a liquid into a gas called water vapor

extinction The dying out of a species

fertile Having or capable of producing an abundance of vegetation or crops

food chain A chain of organisms in which each member uses the member below as food

food web The interlinked food chains in an ecosystem

fungi A kind of organism that absorbs food

glaciers Slow-moving masses of ice

habitat The natural environment of an animal or plant

hardy Able to stand up to harsh conditions

immune Protected from or not responsive to a disease or poison

interdependence A state in which plants and animals rely on each other for survival

interrelationships The relationships between many different organisms and their environment

landscaping Improving the appearance of an area of land by planting trees, shrubs, grass, or flowers

larvae The young, wingless, feeding stage of an insect

lichens Types of organisms made up of fungi and algae living together in a mutualistic relationship

life cycles Changes that take place from the time an organism begins its life until it is an adult that can reproduce

mammals Warm-blooded animals that have lungs, a backbone, and hair or fur, and drink milk from their mother's body

microorganisms Organisms so tiny they can only be seen through microscopes

microscopic So small that it can be seen only by using a microscope

mining The removal of metals, minerals, stone, and other materials from the earth

mutualistic Describing a relationship between two or more species that benefits or helps both species

native Originating from a specific location

nocturnal Active only at night

nutrients Substances that allow organisms to thrive and grow

organisms Living things

parasites Organisms that live in or on other organisms and harm them

photosynthesis The process in which plants use sunlight to change carbon dioxide and water into food and oxygen

phytoplankton Microscopic organisms that live in water and are producers. Zooplankton are another form of microscopic plankton, but they are consumers

pollinate To transfer pollen grains to the part of a plant that reproduces

population The total number of one species in an area

precipitation Water that falls from the clouds as rain, snow, sleet, or hail

predators Animals that hunt other animals for food

prey on To hunt and eat another animal

repopulate To provide a new population

reproduce To produce offspring

reptiles Animals, such as lizards and snakes, that have scales and that rely on the surrounding temperature to warm or cool their bodies

salt ponds Places where standing water, which is a mix of ocean water and fresh water, gathers to form a pond

species A group of animals or plants that are similar and can produce young

symbiosis A relationship between two or more species that benefits or helps both species

undigested Not processed by the digestive system

venom A poisonous fluid found in some animals, such as scorpions and snakes

wilderness An area of land that has not been changed by human activity

Learning More

Find out more about Earth's precious desert ecosystems.

Books

Hyde, Natalie. *Desert Extremes*. New York, NY: Crabtree Publishing Company, 2009.

Waldron, Melanie. *Deserts* (Habitat Survival). Chicago, IL: Raintree Perspectives, 2012.

Latham, Donna. *Deserts*. Norwich, VT: Nomad Press, 2010.

Websites

Visit the website below to learn about some of the careers that you could choose in ecology:
http://kids.nceas.ucsb.edu/ecology/careers.html

Find out more cool facts and tips on ecosystems at:
http://eschooltoday.com/ecosystems/scales-of-an-ecosystem.html

Discover more about deserts and the science of ecosystems at:
www.ducksters.com/science/ecosystems/desert_biome.php

Read lots of fun desert facts at:
http://kids.nceas.ucsb.edu/biomes/desert.html

Index